# Native Instincts

By

Rod Carlos Stryker

Published by
Human Error Publishing
www.humanerrorpublishing.com
paul@humanerrorpublishing.com

Copyright © 2016
by
Human Error Publishing & Rod Carlos Stryker
All Rights Reserved

ISBN: 978-0-9833344-4-6

Front Cover:
Rod Carlos Stryker

Back Cover by
Rod Carlos Stryker

Author's Photograph - page 76
by
Anna Soto

Art Photography by Rod Carlos Stryker:
Land of Saturdays - page 20
Cityscapes - page 28
Brahms, The Hard Way Final - page 38
Wisdom - Page 46
Brahms, The Easy Way Final - page 72

Human Error Publishing asks that no part of this publication be reproduced or transmitted in any form or by any means electronic or mechanical, including photocopy, recording or information storage or retrieval system without permission in writing from Rod Carlos Styker and Human Error Publishing . The reasons for this is to help support the artist.

**This book is dedicated to:**

-Sabina-
pure in your love, true to your nature,
this poet loves you
and aspires to such
heights.

# Table of Contents

| | |
|---|---|
| Butchers of Soy | 6 |
| Bowels Of Heaven | 7 |
| Blood Vein | 8 |
| Certified by Benny | 9 |
| Band-Aids and Cement | 10 |
| Brilliant Bath | 11 |
| Drive-In Catastrophe | 12 |
| Heaven's Gone Missing | 13 |
| Today's Top Stories | 15 |
| Darwin and the Pope | 16 |
| Money, Guns, and Condoms | 17 |
| Road Kill and Neosporin | 19 |
| Land of Saturdays | 21 |
| Blood, Poetry, and Symbiosis | 22 |
| Ted Banes | 23 |
| What It's Like | 24 |
| Top Soil | 25 |
| To April from September | 26 |
| Songs | 27 |
| Sophia Screams | 29 |
| Lilacs Folded | 30 |
| Stars and Buffalo Bones | 31 |
| Dali Waking | 32 |
| Death and Butterfly Kisses | 33 |
| Love is | 34 |
| Drugstore Muses | 35 |
| Death's Prayer | 36 |
| Sour Milk | 37 |
| Brahms, the Hard Way | 39 |
| Reasons That I Write | 40 |
| Where You Lay Your Head | 41 |
| Done | 42 |
| Codex and Totems | 43 |
| Warholy | 44 |
| Fathers and Sons | 45 |
| Wisdom | 47 |
| Flaming Singularity | 48 |

| | |
|---|---|
| Emily | 49 |
| Smother | 50 |
| Season's Soil | 52 |
| After Morning | 53 |
| Morning Newspaper | 54 |
| A Mountain of Ocean | 55 |
| Rust | 56 |
| Sunday Worship | 57 |
| Small Town Hero | 59 |
| The First Woman | 60 |
| CNN and Pepper Spray | 61 |
| Finale | 62 |
| Dandelion Nightmares | 63 |
| Sunflowers and Honey-Do's | 64 |
| Curandera | 65 |
| Columbus Day | 66 |
| Kerosene Dreams | 68 |
| The Well | 70 |
| A Place | 71 |
| Brahms, the Easy Way | 73 |
| | |
| Brief Bio | 77 |
| Acknowledgements | 79 |
| Review | 80 |

## Butchers of Soy

Cows
w/eyes of buttered moons
rejoice
at the sound of
butchers
put out to pasture.

Homogenized
for safety's sake,
they chew cud,
these butchers-of-old,
aprons freshly starched,
gleam in the setting sun
dribbling below the horizon

until twilight reveals
barbecue grills
fired up for pork franks
and soy burgers

## Bowels of Heaven
"It's snowing in the devil's stomach" – Benjamin Peret

A chill
begs pages from
dusty tomes
to describe
itself,
divide,
demarcate,
color the new frost,

paint lost souls found
waving angels
in snow,

saving pearls
in ice boxes,
locked against
TV dinners and frozen peas
in heaven's bowels

## Blood Vein

There's blood in the milk,
spread through like veins
most varicose.

Jagged, ruby lines of
insanity against
the clear glass,

it clings
to the cheerios,

floaters
in a red-scarred sea
of white.

There's blood
in the milk,

and it
refuses to mix.

## Certified by Benny

"her name is Irma and she inspected my shirt"
Robert Pinsky

His name's Benny
and he certified my brake job,

bled the lines
and wrenched the pads
in place,

secured the boot
and tightened the lug nuts,

wiped the rotors down
and tested the brakes himself.

My tires squeal around
a dangerous curve,
at night,
in a torrential storm.

I think how much
I like Benny,

at least until the next
turn's outcome,

should've had the tires replaced…

## Band-Aids and Cement

It frightens her
when he lets the pills
and silence
move his fists

in rapid succession

against the dry-wall
plaster,

paints his knuckles
in bloody anger
flecked
w/hopeless,
white cement.

She wraps his enraged,
scarlet mess
in bandages and tears,
again,

terrified, resigned
to what keeps her
imprisoned

in his pain and
her addiction.

## Brilliant Bath

Doubts flood
tender boardwalks,
crash pleasure craft
against the shore,

spill years
across the beach,
chase
laughter
back into the
surf's cruel thunder.

Sweet regret
buffets palm trees,
dumps cars and buses
into front yards,
against town halls.

Lessons wash
streets clean
before a
sun's brilliant bath.

## Drive-In Catastrophe
(B movie pin-up poem)

My eyes freeze on
her movie-star screams
built on graham crackers
and campy melodramas,
flashed on a populace
of drive-ins doomed
by statuesque, 60's queens

in skin-tight leotards.

The graham crackers spill
on parked cars and couples
frenching on playground
swings, their breath
salted w/popcorn and lust.

The movie screens warp
in Dali-esque shapes that
melt and pour through
neighborhood streets caught
flat-footed by
daily, 9 to 5 currents.

Someone thinks to call
the police too late
as 5th and Main are
flooded under sheets
of movie reels
flowing like the Mississippi

before B movie
rapids crash against
interstate highways.

Wish those svelte, 60's sirens
were here to bring it all into
focus.

## Heaven's Gone Missing

Each day,
a little more of my heaven
goes missing
from your eyes

plays lazy
by the front porch
and wanders down the street,
gazes in confusion
at where to set off next…

anywhere but within
your gaze.

Mornings I try
to recreate
what was lost
by breakfast in bed
or making sweet love
after you wake
in my arms,

still, less clouds remain,
no chance of rain
in the forecast,

just sunny skies
that foretell
barren thoughts
of love
scattered in deserts.

Everyday, more
is missing
from this house

and is laid to rest
the night before,

in the backyard,
lit by
full moon's glow.

The neighbor's dog
tries to dig it up,
but runs and yelps
with tail between legs

from the horror,
bleached white
by Luna's light of

heaven
last seen
in your clear,
sweet eyes.

## Today's Top Stories

God was pulled over for drunk driving.
Local police say the officer who administered a breathalyzer test alleges that the Almighty blew too hard and the device exploded all over the road whereupon the officer attempted to handcuff the Supreme One. All the officer remembers after that is ending up in his patrol car on top of a water tower…upside down.

Also tonight, Congress has decided
to remove the President's executive powers
because, as the legislators' most recent official statement points out, "he doesn't want to play nice." No further details were available but witnesses standing on Pennsylvania Avenue claim they heard a lot of crying and cursing from inside the White House.

In other news, the Hindu god Shiva
was spotted giving a serious "smack-down" to a couple of thieves who thought it was a good idea to steal the Creator/Destroyers wallet. Details are still sketchy, but witnesses say one thief was turned to dust, while the other was turned into a mosquito which alighted on the God/Goddess' arm, She/He then slapped the mosquito to the next life after it tried to bite Him/Her.

And later, we'll talk to a young girl
who claims her pet bunny tells her to kill all infidels hiding in her closet along with a rebuttal from Mr. and Mrs. Infidel who currently live at 2123 Park Ave., suite 9, little girl's closet 2.

These top stories and more when we return…

# Darwin and the Pope

Love's
parting comforts
hang on for weeks
in familiar blossoms,
hung upside down,
grown black
w/age,
grips the wall,
keeps it from
falling against our
pain and anger,
eager to blame
someone, something.

Outside,
Darwin frolics
with the Pope
in idyllic serenity
though certain uncertainties
remain.

And nursing
a tender ego,
I grope
the streets for
chunky
leaps of faith
poured fresh
amid origins of
despair,
content to wait,
patient to see
where your love
falls…next.

## Money, Guns and Condoms

stashed in the top drawer
"Just in case," she says
with a coquettish smirk,
Mona-Lisa style.
I wonder,
in case of what?
But I leave
such questions
back in seedy motel rooms
and 2am street corners,
she needs a wheel man,
right now.
She's ready for another bank job,
says, "it's the last one."
It's always the last one.
But I'm in
the thick of it,
too many bank jobs,
armored car jobs,
convenience store jobs,
there's no backing out
and she won't be denied,
ever.
Learned that early on.
Says she's a Buddhist,
didn't know Buddhists
were into armed robbery.
Maybe they have
Thieving Buddhist Meetings
once a month.
Maybe I should
be a Buddhist.
Nah, couldn't see
myself
staring at walls
for enlightenment.

Money, guns and condoms,
there's my enlightenment,
my faith.

## Road Kill and Neosporin

We'd sledgehammered every molecule of
road kill twice, thrice and then some
until the mention of past grievances made us
growl and bare our teeth.

But in the deepness of night,
we held each other, blessed
in our laughter and tears,

gave each other permission to open
our wounds and slather on
more Neosporin,

a pretense of innocence, if only for a moment.

Soon, we'll forget the road kill
as it disappears
in our rearview mirror.

## Land Of Saturdays
- Oahu -

Every day, Saturday.

When we went to
the Times SuperMarket
last Monday,
ate at the local
L&L Barbeque
two weeks ago
next Friday,
and on Thursday
took in the view at Pali Lookout,

it was Saturday,

Visited the Bishop Museum,
on a windy Sunday,
buried our toes in Bellows beach
w/a hint of secret Wednesdays,
by chance enjoyed the giclee art
at Sunshine Arts Gallery yesterday,

it was still Saturday.

As the clouds kiss the mountain peaks
above the Byodo-In Temple
or the Ko'olau mountains
reflect the morning sun
next year,
next lifetime,

it will still be
the Land of Saturdays.

## Blood, Poetry, and Symbiosis

Her tattoo says "Blood is Poetry!"
w/requisite trails and drops
of blood raining down her leg.

I feel a symbiosis
so intimate, I almost
run to the nearest
tattooist to drill
"Poetry is Pain!"
on my back, arm or other
equally visible
body part when
screaming naked through
Times Square or Piccadilly Circus.
But such hunger

passes and instead,
I hail a taxi
to view the beached
dolphins yelling
haikus to anyone w/in
earshot. Full details
at 5,10 and 11 on CNN.
The oysters sing

backup later in the evening
to Madonna's next incarnation
but I lose interest
and play blues
w/a local band of sea turtles
who insist
on lyrics that include
"Blood is Poetry!"
"Blood is Poetry!"

Yes, a symbiosis
quite intimate.

## Ted Banes
A Thin Line Between Fact and Fiction

Banes lights a cigarette,
the match reflects in his transparent eyes.
He fades in and out of existence,
depending on who you talk to.

Many are convinced
he's right behind them
in a little Honda,
or shadowing a client's
kid,

Pops in and out
of stake outs,
spies on
ex-wives and ex-husbands,
no one gets a good look at
him,
he's quick to disappear.

A real private dick,
like TV gumshoes
in the 30's and 40's.
A shadow, a phantom,
you think you see him,
but you really don't.

Ted Banes, he's that good.

## What It's Like

A pound of flesh for
every syllable,
each consonant.

Two pints of blood
for a vowel, a verb.

A plough to
slice through
muscle and sinew
for a metaphor,
a bit of imagery.

Baked in festered
sanctity,

grown between
loosened
booby traps that
threaten to explode.

Left in the fields
to fend for itself.

This is what it's
like
for a poem,

a poet.

## Top Soil

We barter
intimacy,
play loose and reckless
w/each other's
vocal chords,

excite the
Blue Dog
when bored or
on the verge
of tears.

Suffer in chorus
as forlorn fish
boiling in tonight's
dinner pot
until we cast
off
our mortal coils

for preserved
top soil
farmed against
next season's harvest.

## To April from September

We cross
deltas painted
in deep September,

born in debt
and
Wonder bread dreams,

raised w/picket fence lies
spitting argyle sunsets
across the delta's
gaping mouth

and lend
credence
to counterfeit
horizons.

Let's cross
into clear April rain
and leave
Wonder bread
myths behind.

## Songs

My goddess of song is
a terrified angel
who blots out my eyes
but whispers truth
beached against
the sea.

Gulls cry and sway
at stilted shambling
as I feel
for a purchase
of grass or soil,
anything but
grains of sand
bleeding between fingers.

It's then the angel
asks if I'm a god,

"to create is to breathe is to live"
I counter,

and fall into
the cruel surf,

laugh through the pain
of nascent vistas
in one breath
and blinding light
the next.

I climb out of
the healing tide,
avert Death's gaze,

alive in my
Cantos.

## Sophia Screams

God, the human,
screams in the street,
eviscerates the general air
of raping and pillaging,
a killjoy to the riots.

Her shrieks crescendo
and shatter the mobs,
scatter pieces
along sidewalks
that float between
the Boom! Boom! Boom!
as feathers
fall on
C4 craters
that crumble
in silence.

Paper swords
wave in bonfires,
point towards
playgrounds
burnt and covered
in black soot,
these infernos
flow in graceful
arcs through
shinny summer sun,
flash lightning
into oceans,
concrete, bedrock.

God's cries disappear
into autumn blooms
amid white doves,
motionless,
calm.

## Lilacs Folded

Children of the sun
play in lilacs
blown through golden
pages folded
clean and clear,

take up silences
night would covet,

blanket coliseums
sporting
screams and howls
legion disguises
as human.

We origami these
unforgiving parodies
the Piper trills for,
rats and vermin biting
at his heals,

and one is labeled
rouser of rabble,
subversive,

poet.

## Stars and Buffalo Bones

W/in a circle of uneasy shouts,
paper children
fold themselves in shapes
of stars, snakes and buffalo bones.

The lighthouse
blinds their efforts,
but they continue
through eyes slit
and songs that
rival choirs of angels

even as melodramatic fish
snag their mouths on their
own fishing poles,
reel themselves in
just to enjoy
something different

than paper children
and blinding
houses lit
w/portents and
fickle hearts

that spell an end
to this circle of shouting,
snakes and buffaloes bent
through origami rituals
absent of color,
of stars.

## Dali Waking

She ends at the beginning,
paints the walls
blueberry beige
before sopping up the spills
w/crackers and submarine sam'iches.

I tell her to add more mayo,
but she holds the mustard instead,
wails about pickles and poetry
getting in the carpet
then swan dives off the love seat
into the pool table
that holds catfish
and cod.

I pull her off the reef
before the storm hits,
the one that's been hanging around the ceiling
since yesterday.

Fortunately, the boat I rented
last week makes it to the side pocket
before the real downpour
floods August all over January.

We dry off
w/sardines and condiments
placed next to the coffee table
and begin at the end, again.

## Death and Butterfly Kisses

As the band plays our
feverish butterfly kisses,
the devil barters
finite smiles

w/lost corruption
until the surreal killings
she commits
atones a mountain
of innocence,

penance for the Duke of Death
who gathers flowers and tears

next to nightmares of jump-rope
and hopscotch.

We rest on sensual haunches
sweaty w/saucy goodness
before pressing equine smiles
against butterfly kisses.

# Love is

…spring water
mixed w/spirits
shaken and stirred
w/Satan's horn
and the Goddess feather.

…autumn zephyr
boiled in Aphrodite's thong
while foaming
down a hurricane's throat
before filling up
a rose petal chalice
poised against
good intentions
and movie star dramas.

…winter soil
peppered w/indecision
and bled down
sacrifice's face
wiped against
longing's legs
and tossed
into the laundry
w/no hope of
ever coming clean.

Love is…

## Drugstore Muses

I hear the sound
of muses bodily
hit the page,
leap-frog over each other
just to get the last word in
while I sweat through
my jockey shorts
desperate for
a science to explain
the trembling mouth
screaming through
grey matter
scrambled to a fine froth.

I untie the strings
attached through my
ears,
fumble w/theories
that surround
sacred trees and pickled dreams
left in the sun,
ripened and gathered
by mercurial cogitators.

Exhausted,
I tempt
battered and beaten
epiphanies,
still waging
war on paper,
w/rare glimpses
of insight sold
at the corner drugstore
for a buck fifty.
Yeah, inflation's
a bitch.

# Death's Prayer

"And in the end, we prayed for death – Judy Reeves"

And in the beginning
Death prays for us,
drops a spark of insight
in our infant dreams,
pulls all-night vigils
praying we make it
to see the dawn,
a birthday,
a lifetime
measured in centuries,
not decades.

The Dark Angel tumbles
right along side,
a shadow we ignore
until tragedy
or some random
accident reminds us
of mortal coils
and fragile lives
sluiced between
streams of bills
and taxes.

In the end,
the Reaper
stops praying
long enough to collect
our tattered souls
as She ponders
the next spark
will put Her
out of a job.

## Sour Milk

There's a change in the milk
soured by famine
and Arab springtime

coupled w/rising tides
warmed over
global proportions.

But change con leche
might wean
mass murderers
from Knights Templar

if only
faux news
would let loose
its gauntlet full

of hate.

And fate plays
fast and easy

among cattle calls
of blind crowds
singing to drown out

children begging
for a morsel of food,
a few drops of
sour milk.

# Brahms, the Hard Way

Tobacco-chewin' curse-slingin' hard-lookin'
biker bum forces
his way into the matinee,
grabs popcorn and candy bars
and slaps the movie ushers
right in their pimply faces
then howls during
Lord of the Rings
or Harry Potter parts 1 through 8,
makes passes
at the girl w/the cello
in the concert hall as
the symphony
struggles through Brahms.

Wise-crackin' fish-smellin' middle-fingerin'
the cops who make the mistake
of trying to arrest him
before he shoots out their tires
and holes up in the warehouse
district until he decides
to invade Canada
w/foul ideas of conservative
politics and random acts of mayhem.

Beer-swillin' gun-firin' dead-pilin'
higher than a garbage scow towed
out to New York's Staten Island
as the seagulls cry and scream
for mercy from
his lead-filled onslaught
coupled w/helping old ladies
across the street just to
leave them in the middle
lane during rush hour traffic-

Shit, I love Brahms.

## Reasons That I Write

because tears
need a witness in the rain

and the homeless
need a voice in the silence

to open hope's eyes
for one more day of what-could-be

if a child
begs for love with her eyes

when a people
rise up for what is right

or a mom
takes a third job to make ends meet

will the bluebonnets
paint the fields in azul tones

if the breath
creates the life para darnos el amor

and the meaning
gets lost and found within

the always growing reasons
that I write and write and write

## Where You Lay Your Head

Today we woke up in a plaid house
decked out w/Roman chariots
as couches
and breast plates doubled
as art on the walls.

Last week we went to sleep
surrounded by Egyptian hieroglyphics
for wallpaper and
pyramids that grew
out of the headboards.

Tomorrow perhaps
NASCAR will put us
to sleep w/the
susurrated drone of
150 mile-an-hour
cars spinning around
our heads.

Next week may give
us a tender moment
as we perch atop the highest peak
on IO as it
circles Jupiter
over and over again.

# Done
-Occupy Planet Earth-

Are we done footing the bill,
then have said feet
shoved in our mouths
if we object
or protest treatment
no better
than sheep to slaughter
by privileged owners
who count coins
and bet on
the 99% never
standing up
for inalienable human
rights?

Are we done...folding,
caving to those
who put us out
in the dead of winter
careless, shameless
in their actions
that effect thousands
just for the bottom line?

Are we done...kneeling,
bowing to allow for
wealth-clad shoes
to stand on sore shoulders,
trod on stooped
backs scarred
by the whip,
hate, and indifference?

Are we done...?

## Codex and Totems

The Mixtec Codex
plows behind my eyes
and through a bed of roses
around her waist
painted in Rauschenberg red,
held between
top-hat monkeys
and dancing skeletons.

We sound the bells
for the little people
living in my earlobes
who simultaneously
drown out
the funny folk
behind the glass.

The trophy horn announces
ceremonial rituals
involving Diadem crowns
and caged bears
as swaddled,
sculpted children
construct totems
in my brain
until the codex
slams shut.

## Warholy

Plastic soup cans
are electrified for
Mao's pleasure
amid cowboys and
Liza Minnelli.

We have guns
that shoot Liberty
while Lupe sleeps,
head cushioned by
the tidy-bowel man.

My Brillo pads
scrub the last
vestiges of Empire
clean of painted
Marilyns and dead Jackies.

We kneel beneath
the neon Jesus
in hopes of saving
our collective,
pop-culture souls.

## Fathers and Sons

Named them at birth
in tears and mirth,
embraced
w/strong arms of
muscle and bone,
but stretched to breaking,
pulled and forsaking
fathers and sons.

Babies and drama
cradle the heart
out of chests
as backbones remain
straight and unbroken,
blocks any token
of connection and fusion
w/fathers and sons.

Twisted by hate,
blind to a faith
of acceptance and inclusion,
destined to ruin
love and truth
between fathers and sons.

# Wisdom

She is worshiped
as necessary,
fills memories
previously perished
where lands end
and stars begin,
cloying scent
and lace
curls and rolls
as waves and rivers
past gray bones
weeping for a second
chance to gather
Her summer nights
between clutching
fingers,
they gasp for air
frozen in beatitude
to Her divinity
as storms
rage and thunder
just beneath Her
pale cheeks
and Her smiling,
rose-painted
lips.

Skies draw back
and bow
to Her passing,
crash into
oceans of galaxies
and stars,
and all I can utter is:
"fuck."

## Flaming Singularity

A sweet flame rages
beneath my heart,
sings to me at night,
bathes me in
sweat and fire
and incandescent light.

My skull explodes
as the muse's words
are blown to
all points between
Buenos Aires and Alpha Centauri,

but I move the pain
off my furrowed brow
and refuse Serendipity
one last time
before a black hole

swallows my soul,
the Earth, and all
those playgrounds
of childhood memories
w/nothing left,
except a mackerel sky.

# Emily
for Emily Dickinson

She screamed in black fog,
the sound died quickly,
her words
"I'm Nobody, who are you?"

plowed through her
throat to no avail
until her nose bled
and her voice
grew hoarse
and the fog
folded
as she fell
supine on asphalt.

I finally approached
through white fog
and crouched where
she lay,
panting her words
over and again,

"I'm somebody, I know you,"
I murmured, smiled
and laid my hand
on her forehead
until she opened
her eyes.

"Ok, poet." she whispered
and smiled, too.

## Smother
for B.K.S.

Her cancer leaves me
crushed
by its prickly scent,

brushes against my nose,
my face,
every pore,

raises the hairs on my neck,
bathes me in rusty dread

threatens to suffocate.

I choke down
the pain

that has leveled her
to this charcoal-sealed
apartment
behind dumpsters
and recrimination,

begins to burn
just beneath
my lucidity,

boils all sense
save guilt and
house cleaning:

until I take a breath,
place guilt and broom
back in the closet.

I sit with
her
and her cancer,

take pleasure in
coffee and hope.

## Season's Soil

Don that soil
loosened from last night's
downpour.

Rub this earth
deep into skin
bled through clothes
newly starched.

Pat those stones
beneath feet
scarred from million
mile walks on asphalt memories.

Rest these fields
amid amber suns
and cobalt skies,
silent as a Goddess whisper.

# After Morning

After *After Midnight* by Louis Simpson

The lit roads are swollen
with traffic and a morning sun,
harsh with alarms waking.

As all horns blare, full and loud,
in the front yard, kids scream
at new days, and success.

Who drives all these noisy cars?
As the smog becomes self-aware,
I could choke on all its fumes.

The crossing guard returns
to this side of the road,
cursing slowly under his breath.

## Morning Newspaper

Rolled up the morning
in newspaper
like one should

to keep it fresh

w/featured stories
of black flowers
singing sailor songs

in top hats
and mascara
last night,

a lovely arrangement of
Civil War southern bells
who sashay
from left to right

and sprinkle
rodent laughter

over plague politics.

Current events
hitches a ride home,
bone tired

from all the sailor songs
and political
tumors,

head full
of evergreen visions
sporting Lincoln

and black, top hat
flowers.

## A Mountain of Ocean

I huddle
on the shore
by the mountain
w/her grief
in my pocket,

fierce waves
salt my toes clean
of loose guilt.

Reasons explode
against her rejection,

it flows between
impotent complaints
I sputter to evoke,
but the mountain wins,

crumbles over my
best intentions
until her grief
is all that's left.

## Rust

Tired of rust stains
scattered across
my heart,
my soul.
No amount
of Rust-Away
cleanses the flaws,
I stopped writhing

in anger
and frustration
years ago at these
bronze-colored
shapes, blobs,
and streaks.
They've hardened into scars
and knots, merged

into each other
and grown,
closer to the center.
Denial is a luxury

for the lazy and the dead.
My rust lives and is
real as rain, trees,

and love.

## Sunday Worship

At Tia Carmen's:

Family, rice,
cousins, uncles, aunts,
red kidney beans,
and sibling rivalry
all vie for attention,
demand dysfunction,
aromas drift carelessly
through house and senses.

Tosinos for niños
and sneaky adults,
avocado lined up
in crescent-shaped wedges,
hurtful looks and arguments,
all presage
the main attraction,

a generational dish
crossing years
and oceans and wars.
Served with pride
and varied recipes,
Pernil,
is butter on
tongue and taste buds
if cooked
by Tia Carmen's standards
that include
the freshest garlic,
ground pepper, oregano,
and more,

a Boriqua-born homage
to the Isle of Enchantment.

Brief as this

congregation is,
we recall our
family roots,

join in worship
around the dinner table.

## Small Town Hero

punch that clock,
fumble home,
stale crackers
for nourishment,

bottomless sleep
for 2 hours,
alarm blasts
anxiety awake,

slog to work
in scarcely clean clothes,
heart hides
down that rabbit hole,

another 16 hours
of scrapping
the barrel's bottom
deemed a poverty life,

doesn't seem heroic.

# The First Woman

Where is it written
that I must lay beneath
him?

Wonders and paradise
lie before us,
we trod the dust
we're made from,
side by side,
yet he exhorts
his role on top.

Woman and man,
goddess and god,
a glorious eternity
as two sides
of one coin.

But now
the Father has judged
my husband's right
to rule over
me, proclaim
privilege above me,
violate my freedoms
on top of me!

It is clear
not Adam,
God, nor Paradise
are worthy
of me.

I am
Lilith.

## CNN and Pepper Spray

Today, the pepper spray was strong,
clouded my eyes
in film and pain,

still can't open them
much.

Yesterday, a rubber bullet
pierced Mai Li's shoulder,
we jury-rigged a sling,

glad the bleeding stopped.

Tomorrow, Kwan will bring food,
a relief from fasting,
since last night,

this protesting is hungry
work.

Tonight, I hope to survive
the policeman's baton,
a government's betrayal

for a chance it might air on CNN.

# Finale

it's a punch line
held by the dusk

if anxiety hadn't
splashed its nervous

laughter all over
the gashed sky

who is luminous, furious
at the sun's disregard

for order or gravity
while the sea gets

married to bed sheets
in steamy hours

way past reasonable,
and fingers

run under chins and smiles
soaked in memory,

simmered in apprehension
and torrents of pure blue.

# Dandelion Nightmares

Fierce sleep
engulfs the supine
form of my
landscape

with trees that
weep and hills
that run between
dandelions
and streams.

Rivers scamper along
banks too steep
for polite nightmares
and instead

pretend roaring
daydreams that rain
misty rivulets
and fierce, supine
sleep.

## Sunflowers and Honey-Do's

Grab those
suspenders wrapped
'round my legs,
faded and worn,
snaps creaky
from years of use

Untie these
sunflowers stitched
in my hair,
drooping and dying,
by years and use.

Throw that
'shroom hat
clutched in my mouth
against ol' Stars and Stripes
'cuz she forgets
our tears and honey-do's.

## Curandera

Swings her gaze
any other way but
dead in the eye,
she's always on point,
casts spells below
the radar, pays it forward
lessons she's learned
in Mexican witchcraft and
schoolyard bullies. Swings her
games through bullshit
and dreams, breaks noses and hearts
in random order, fakes concern
for the burn of little lies and stars
that churn in her mind, her heart tossed
in the oil spills corporately corrupted,
she can never swing too harsh against moneyed
murders and bloodied hands grouped
by betrayal and broken promises...

# Columbus Day

Boricu'a saw the ships
with white cloths
like clouds, these

ships brought men
who spoke ugly
noise, like iguaca.

The ugly,
upright animals seemed
as gods, at first.

Some of us lacked
trust in their
shiny clothes

and their buticaco eyes.
They did not
honor the Bo'jike.

Then the cacike
tested one of
these gods, and drowned

him. He stayed dead.
Now, Bohiti warns
of guazabara

as our bohios burn,
we make ready
to fight the evil

leader they call Columbus.

Taino (Puerto Rican Indigenous People) Language Key:

Boricu'a - The Valiant People of the Sacred House
iguaca - green parrot
buticaco - shifty eyes
Bo'jike - Great Lord of the Forest and Earth
cacike - Chief
Bohiti - shaman - a Taino spiritual leader
guazabara - war, warrior
bohios - roundhouses

**Kerosene Dreams**
for Dr. Martin Luther King, Jr.

The Molotov cocktail
screams past,
look back,
see history,

fought and paid
with blood and lives,

not with thugs
de jour for
reasons forgotten
between burning
families and

childish tears
streaming faces

lost to innocence,
damned to nightmares
running down streets.
Look back,

see Martin's dream
burn beneath

Gestapo pyres reeking
of kerosene, Ferguson,
Baltimore, North Charleston,
and mountain tops
falling, falling.

Look back,
dance on no more graves

swaddled in sacrifice,
in struggle.
Let the fires
go out.

Look back.

## The Well

Nothing but sand,
a mountain of granules
that gathers
deep within.

Slight moisture
collects
w/evening's chill,
but disappears
against another's
dry lips
while more sand

swells and waits for
distant Spring rains.

# A Place

to hold my light-skinned grandson
without suspicion or police presence,

...to give my light-skinned wife a kiss without
public eyes that caress hate all over me

...to stride on a sidewalk
without fearful glances or mistrust

...to return home without
being interrogated because of my dark skin

...where dark skin is celebrated and not
treated with a nightstick or a bullet to the head

...I can look to with pride and love
and peace and joy and and and...
no more war

...Some where,
some

place.

## Brahms, the Easy Way

Left the warehouse district,
lost one too many against the cops,
southbound with the girl
playing her cello,
she still struggles with Brahms.

Breaking speed limits,
dead set on easing into
the Fates hands
before he steals their
baleful scissors,
cuts the string himself,

splayed against neon signs
that foretell his demise,
our hero smiles
hurtling with car, cello, and Brahms
blasting towards the sky.

## Brief Bio for Rod C. Stryker

Rod C. Stryker has been writing for over 30 years. His first book, Exploits of a Sun Poet (Pecan Grove Press, February 2003), was awarded the San Antonio Barnes and Noble/Bookstop Author-of-the-Month, February 2003 and also the San Antonio Current Best Book of 2005. His 2nd collection of poetry and art photography, Lucid Affairs, was published by Sun Arts Press. Rod began the Sun Poetic Times literary-visual arts magazine in 1994, founded the Sun Poet's Society in 1995 and co-founded the Sun Arts Foundation in 2004. The Sun Poet's Society is known today around the world and celebrated its 20th Anniversary in March 2015. Rod mentors people of all ages, backgrounds and genres and he was nominated for the San Antonio Poet Laureate in April 2012 and April 2014.

Rod started photography as illustrations for his poetry in Exploits of a Sun Poet, Lucid Affairs, and Native Instincts. However, his photographs have taken on a life of their own. His art photography shows have been held at such galleries as Blue Star Arts Complex, Casa Chiapas and Ruta Maya, Riverwalk in San Antonio, Texas.

# Acknowledgements:

Some of the poems that appear in this book have also been previously published:

Brilliant Bath,
Smother,
A Mountain of Ocean,
Published in
Lucid Affairs by Rod Carlos Stryker (Sun Arts Press)

Rust - San Antonio Express News
Land of Saturdays - Voices De La Luna Magazine
Lilacs Folded - Austin International Poetry Festival Anthology 2012
Songs - Austin International Poetry Festival Anthology 2013
Emily - Austin International Poetry Festival Anthology 2014
Season's Soil - Austin International Poetry Festival Anthology 2015
Done - 99 Poems for the 99 Percent Anthology

# Reviews

A beautiful power edging on pain, Stryker's "Native Instincts" reveals a sensitivity wrought from years of experience and experiences, a wisdom built from the sweat and muscles, grief and survival skills of Desert Storm and workaday America. His "Kerosene Dreams" dedicated to M. L. K. Jr...is a "history... damned to nightmares ...and Gestapo pyres reeking of kerosene... and mountain tops falling, /falling." _____and an admonition to "dance on no more graves/swaddled in sacrifice,/in struggle./Let the fires/go out. /Look back."

This book, a song of symbiosis with the beer-swillin' biker-bum and Brahms, with beached dolphins yelling haikus and terrified angels blinding us, with "Band-Aids and Cement", is also a song of human survival and a loving connection that embraces the whole of our universe. Stryker has proven here in these poems that he is, indeed, "alive,/in my Cantos."

**Dr. Carmen Tafolla, Texas Poet Laureate 2015**

www.ingramcontent.com/pod-product-compliance
Lightning Source LLC
Chambersburg PA
CBHW051703090426
42736CB00013B/2513